THE CHIPPEWA

A **TRUE BOOK**®

by
Christin Ditchfield

Children's Press®
A Division of Scholastic Inc.

New York Toronto London Auckland Sydney
Mexico City New Delhi Hong Kong
Danbury, Connecticut

A beautifully decorated
Chippewa vest

Content Consultant
Liz Sonneborn

*The photograph on the title
page shows No-Tin, a
Chippewa chief who lived in
the 1800s*

Library of Congress Cataloging-in-Publication Data
Ditchfield, Christin.
   The Chippewa / by Christin Ditchfield.
      p. cm. — (A true book)
   Includes bibliographical references and index.
   0-516-22817-X (lib. bdg.)   0-516-25588-6 (pbk.)
   1. Ojibwa Indians—Social life and customs—Juvenile literature.
2. Ojibwa Indians—History—Juvenile literature. I. Title. II. Series.
E99.C6D58 2005
977.004'97333—dc22   2004030520

CHILDREN'S PRESS, and A TRUE BOOK™, and associated logos are
trademarks and/or registered trademarks of Scholastic Library Publishing.
SCHOLASTIC and associated logos are trademarks and/or registered
trademarks of Scholastic Inc.

1 2 3 4 5 6 7 8 9 10 R 14 13 12 11 10 09 08 07 06 05

Contents

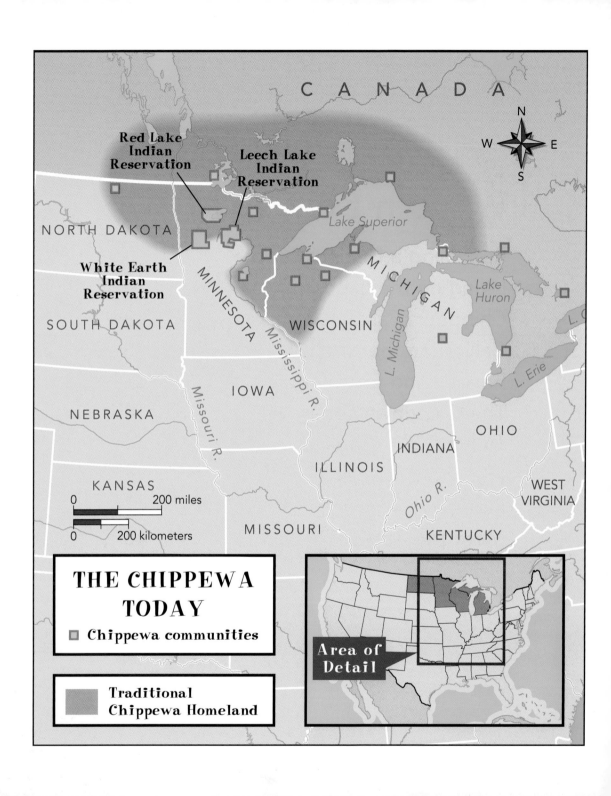

C A N A D A

Red Lake
Indian
Reservation

Leech Lake
Indian
Reservation

Lake Superior

NORTH DAKOTA

MICHIGAN

White Earth
Indian
Reservation

MINNESOTA

Mississippi R.

Lake
Huron

SOUTH DAKOTA

WISCONSIN

L. Michigan

L. Erie

NEBRASKA

IOWA

Missouri R.

OHIO

INDIANA

ILLINOIS

Ohio R.

KANSAS

0   200 miles

0   200 kilometers

MISSOURI

KENTUCKY

WEST
VIRGINIA

THE CHIPPEWA
TODAY

☐ Chippewa communities

Area of
Detail

Traditional
Chippewa Homeland

N
W   E
S

Becoming a Distinct People

The Great Lakes region of North America has been home to American Indians for centuries. Algonquian people settled in villages in parts of Minnesota, North Dakota, Michigan, and Canada. These villages formed larger farming communities.

As time went on, the Algonquian people formed different tribes. Each tribe had its own **culture** and language. Some of them moved away from the Great Lakes. They traveled from place to place to find food, good hunting grounds, and warm weather. By the 1600s, this way of life gave them the name People of the Plains. Other Algonquian people chose to remain near the Great Lakes.

6

The sun sets over Lake Superior, one of the five Great Lakes.

One of the largest and most powerful tribes became known as the Chippewa or Ojibway.

Both of these names come from a word meaning "puckered up," which describes the way their **moccasins** were sewn together at the top. The Chippewa often called themselves *Anishinaabe*, which means "first people."

By the 1700s, the Chippewa had moved north of Lake Huron and northeast of Lake Superior. Their territory included parts of what are now Michigan, Wisconsin,

A group of Chippewa go around Saint Anthony Falls in Minnesota.

Minnesota, North Dakota, Montana, and Oklahoma. They also lived in Ontario, Manitoba, Alberta, and Saskatchewan in Canada.

Living on the Land

The Chippewa used birch bark or mats made of **cattail** leaves to make cone-shaped homes called wigwams. Frames made of arched poles gave the homes their shape. Twine or strips of leather were used to tie the covering together. The Chippewa also lived in tents called tepees.

Tepees were made of birch bark, buckskin, or cloth stretched over long wooden poles. These

Chippewa men hunted deer and other animals for food.

homes could be put up or taken down quickly when the tribe needed to move on.

Chippewa men hunted for deer, moose, bear, elk, and rabbit. Other **prey** included otter, beaver, and mink. Bows and arrows and snares, or traps, were used to catch and kill these animals. The Chippewa also fished from canoes in the Great Lakes and nearby rivers.

The Chippewa used canoes to fish in lakes and rivers.

Wild Rice

Every summer, the Chippewa gathered wild rice, a kind of edible grass seed. It could be found along the banks of lakes, rivers, and streams. They used the rice to make many kinds of cereals, soups, and stews. It was a very important food for the tribe.

Wild rice could be easily stored for use during the winter months when other foods were hard to find.

Chippewa women fill birch bark containers with maple syrup made from the sap of maple trees.

Chippewa women gathered nuts, berries, and wild rice. In the spring, they harvested maple sap to make syrup and sugar. In the summer, they grew corn, beans, pumpkins, and squash.

A group of Chippewa men in traditional clothing

In hot weather, the Chippewa wore light clothing made of green leaves and fibers from nettle stalks. In cold weather, men wore shirts and leggings made of animal skins. They also wore breechcloths—clothing that resembled an apron, with front and back flaps that hung from the waist. Women wore leggings and long dresses. Their dresses were often beautifully decorated with beads, paint, and porcupine quills. In addition, the Chippewa traded with French **settlers** for cloth blankets, which they then made into hooded coats and capes.

Chippewa Family Life

The birth of a baby was cause for celebration among the Chippewa. They believed that every child born into the tribe was a gift to the whole community. Everyone in the tribe was expected to help raise the children. Chippewa children were taught to show respect

All the adults of the tribe helped to raise Chippewa children.

for others by listening to them. They learned that arguing or criticizing others was considered rude. Members of the tribe were expected to think before they spoke.

19

The Chippewa worked hard to care for one another. The men taught the boys how to hunt and how to fight to protect the tribe. Chippewa women taught the girls how to cook and sew and take care of their homes. Everyone did their part to help the tribe survive, and those who had more wealth were expected to share with those who had less.

Although Chippewa life was hard, it was not all work. The

Four Chippewa men play a moccasin game.

people found time to laugh
and play and sing. They
enjoyed all kinds of games.

They loved arts and crafts. Tribe members often sewed beautiful designs on their clothing or carved fancy details onto their tools and toys.

The Chippewa are expert craftspeople who often sew detailed designs on their clothing and other items, such as this bag.

Chippewa men perform a war dance.

Dances were performed as part of Chippewa religious ceremonies. Each ceremonial dance had its own special steps and movements. Children learned to do the dances by watching their parents and grandparents.

Storytelling was a skill that the Chippewa treasured. Some of the best storytellers were women. They would often act out the stories as the tales were told. The tribe had no written language, so the young Chippewa learned their tribal and family histories by listening to older people tell stories about the past.

Naw-gaw-nab was the second
chief of the Wisconsin Chippewa
and an excellent storyteller.

Calling on the Creator

The Chippewa shared a deep faith in the Creator God, whom they called *Kitche Manitou*. They believed this Great Spirit would give them health and happiness if they honored him.

According to Chippewa tradition, Kitche Manitou created the world in stages.

Many objects made by the Chippewa, such as this hand drum, were decorated with pictures of animals. American Indians have great respect for all living things.

First he formed rock, water, fire, and wind. He used these to make the sun, the moon, the stars, and Earth. Then he made plants, animals, and people.

The Chippewa called the sun the father of all living things and Earth the mother of all living things. They believed that all people should live in harmony with nature and the spirit world.

Some tribe members became part of the *Midewiwin* or Grand Medicine Society. These men and women were called *Mides*. They learned how to use plants and herbs to cure sickness. They carried medicine bundles, pouches

A Chippewa medicine man, or mide, holds a ceremonial turtle clan drum.

filled with **sacred** objects, that were thought to have special powers. Mides looked for spiritual guidance through visions and dreams.

As groups of European settlers moved into Chippewa territory,

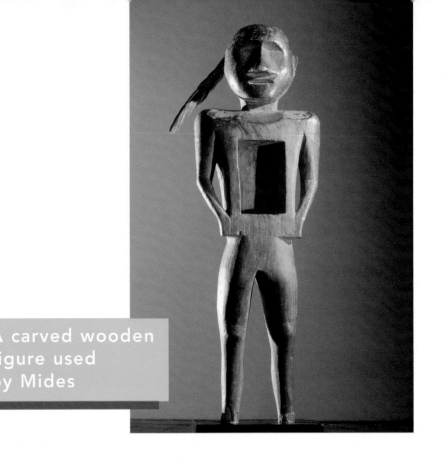

A carved wooden
figure used
by Mides

they brought their own religious
beliefs and customs. The Chippewa
adopted some of these beliefs
and combined them with their
traditional faith to create the
religion that they practice today.

Friends and Enemies

In the early 1600s, the Chippewa came into contact with French explorers around the Great Lakes. They formed friendly relationships with these explorers as well as with the fur traders, **missionaries**, and settlers who followed them. Many Chippewa women learned to

Jean Nicolet (below right, wearing hat with arms upraised) was a French explorer and the first European to see Lake Michigan and present-day Wisconsin.

speak French. They helped the French settlers communicate with Chippewa tribal leaders.

Chippewa men often served as guides for hunters, trappers, and traders. In return, the Chippewa received clothing, tools, and guns. The Chippewa became wealthy and powerful. They expanded their territory and drove other tribes out.

In the 1700s, European nations often fought for control of the eastern part of North America. The Chippewa sided with France against Great Britain during the conflict that became known as the French and Indian War. Great Britain defeated France in this war. During the American Revolution and the War of 1812, the Chippewa sided with the British against the United States. When the United States won, they forced the Chippewa to sign peace treaties and surrender much of their land. The Chippewa agreed to move to reservations, areas of land set aside for them by the U.S. government.

"The Song of Hiawatha"

Jane Johnston Schoolcraft, the daughter of a Chippewa woman and a Scots-Irish fur trader, lived in the early 1800s. Jane wrote beautiful poems about her love of nature, faith, and family. Her husband, Henry, wrote a history of the Chippewa. The Schoolcrafts' writings inspired author Henry Wadsworth Longfellow (above) to pen the famous poem "The Song of Hiawatha." It tells the story of an Indian hero sent by the Great Spirit to guide the nations in the ways of peace. Although Longfellow based his poem on Chippewa legends, the real Hiawatha was an Iroquois.

The U.S. government took more and more Chippewa land as time went on. It did not keep its promises to pay for the land, provide for the people, or respect their rights. In 1968, Chippewa leaders Clyde Bellecourt, Dennis Banks, and George Mitchell founded the American Indian Movement (AIM). They organized protests against the government, complaining of the unfair treatment their people had received. They called on the government to

AIM activists Dennis Banks (left) and Clyde Bellecourt (right) participate in a rally in South Dakota in 1999.

keep its promises. Because of their courage and commitment, life became better for American Indians everywhere.

The Chippewa Today

Today, the Chippewa remain one of the largest Indian tribes in North America. There are more than 100,000 Chippewa in the United States. Most of them still live on or near the reservations in Michigan, Wisconsin, Minnesota, North Dakota, Montana, and Oklahoma.

Students from Lac Courte Oreilles High School ice fish on a lake. The Lac Courte Oreilles Chippewa Reservation in Wisconsin is home to nearly 3,000 Chippewa.

In Canada, more than 60,000 Chippewa live on reserves, or reservations, in Ontario, Manitoba, Alberta, and Saskatchewan.

A girl studies the Chippewa language at an elementary school in Hayward, Wisconsin.

Some members of the tribe work as doctors, lawyers, or engineers. Some are farmers or fishers. Others operate camp-grounds and tourist attractions. They own restaurants, hotels, and other businesses. In many ways, the Chippewa live just like other North Americans.

While living their modern lives, however, the Chippewa try to preserve the history and culture of their tribe. They want their children to understand where they have come from and what it means to be Chippewa. Parents and grandparents work especially hard to pass on the Chippewa language to the next **generation**.

There are newspapers and magazines that celebrate the Chippewa way of life. Even new technology can help members of the tribe preserve their past. Web sites and online groups help many Chippewa connect with one another to share their history and culture.

Each year, hundreds of tribe members gather at Indian festivals. They perform ceremonial songs and dances. They share traditional arts and crafts and recipes. Rodeos and parades

A young girl celebrates her heritage by wearing traditional Chippewa clothing.

are also part of the festivities. By participating in these events, the Chippewa people celebrate their past, present, and future.

To Find Out More

Here are some additional resources to help you learn more about the Chippewa:

 **Books**

Adare, Sierra. **Ojibwe: Native American Peoples.** Gareth Stevens, 2003.

Green, Jacqueline D. **The Chippewa: A First Book.** Franklin Watts, 1999.

Miller, Jay. **American Indian Families.** Children's Press, 1996.

Miller, Jay. **American Indian Festivals.** Children's Press, 1996.

Van Laan, Nancy. **Shingebiss: An Ojibwe Legend.** Houghton-Mifflin Company, 2002.

Williams, Suzanne. **Ojibwe Indians.** Heinemann Library, 2003.

💡 Organizations and Online Sites

National Museum of the American Indian
Fourth Street and Independence Avenue SW
Washington, DC 20024
202-633-1000
http://www.nmai.si.edu/

Visit the museum to learn more about American Indian history and culture.

NativeTech
www.nativetech.org/games

Visit this site to play games that will help you learn more about the Chippewa people or to learn about traditional American Indian toys.

The Red Lake Nation
www.redlakenation.org

This is the official site of the Red Lake band of Chippewa Indians. It has information about the tribe's history and links to information about businesses that are owned by the Red Lake tribe.

The Sault Sainte Marie Tribe of Chippewa Indians
www.sootribe.org

This official site of the Sault Sainte Marie Chippewa has information about the tribe's history, organization, and government.

Important Words

cattail a tall, thin plant with furry brown seed pods at the top

culture the way of life of a group of people

edible able to be eaten safely

generation people born during a certain time

missionary a person who travels to another place to share faith and do good works

moccasins soft leather shoes

prey animals that are hunted for food

sacred holy; having to do with religion; something deserving of great respect

settler a person who moves to a new area and builds a home there

Index

Meet the Author

Christin Ditchfield is an author, conference speaker, and host of the nationally syndicated radio program *Take It to Heart!* Her articles have been featured in magazines all over the world. A former elementary school teacher, Christin has written more than thirty books for children on a wide range of topics, including sports, science, and history. She makes her home in Sarasota, Florida.